P9-ELR-830

Nature's Children

OWLS

Elin Kelsey

FACTS IN BRIEF

Classification of North American owls

Class: *Aves* (birds)
Order: *Stringiformes* (owls)
Family: *Strigidae* (typical owls)
Tytonidae (barn owls)
Species: 18 species found in North America

World distribution. Depends on species. Owls are found world-wide, except in polar regions.

Distinctive physical characteristics. Very large eyes which point forward; ring of curved feathers surrounding each eye.

Habitat, Habits, Diet. Vary with species.

Most common North American species. Barred Owl, Long-Eared Owl, Boreal Owl, Pygmy Owl, Burrowing Owl, Saw-Whet Owl, Elf Owl, Screech Owl, Great Gray Owl, Short-Eared Owl, Great Horned Owl, Snowy Owl, Hawk Owl, North American Barn Owl.

Published originally as
"Getting to Know . . . Nature's Children."

This series is approved and recommended by the Federation of Ontario Naturalists.

This library reinforced edition is available exclusively from:

Grolier Educational Corporation
Sherman Turnpike, Danbury, Connecticut 06816

Contents

Wise old owls probably appear in more cartoons, storybooks, songs and advertisements than any other bird in the world. They seldom have starring roles, however. Mostly they perch on the sidelines looking serious and handing out good advice.

How did owls get their reputation for being so wise? Well, their large eyes always seem to be studying things. And the rings around their eyes remind us of the big, round glasses professors are often pictured wearing. In other words, they *look* wise.

But the truth about real owls is that they are no wiser than any of our other feathered friends!

Masterminds or not, owls are amazing birds. If you would like to know more about them, come read along.

Great Gray Owl

Who's Who?

Owls are found everywhere on earth, except in polar regions. From desert to forest to Arctic tundra, there is at least one type of owl for every habitat.

No matter where they live, owls are easy birds to identify. From the tiny Elf and Saw-Whet owls to the giant Great Gray and Snowy, owls look so much alike that even a beginning bird watcher can tell when he has spotted one.

Like all birds, owls have feathers, hollow bones and young that hatch from eggs. Yet owls are different from other birds in so many ways that they belong to their own special order of birds.

Most of us think of owls as rather large birds, and indeed, many are. Some, however, are no bigger than sparrows. The wee fellow you see here is a Saw-Whet. Tiny as it is, the Elf and Pygmy owls are smaller still.

Fluffy Feathers

From the top of their legs to the edge of their beaks, owls are covered in fluffy feathers. Some owls even have a thick layer of feathers all the way down to the tips of their toes. Owl feathers can be so soft that if you were to close your eyes and feel them, you could easily mistake them for fur.

Most owls have dark gray and brown markings on their feathers. These colors blend in well with their surroundings, and an owl that is sitting still is very hard to spot. So owls that hunt at night—as most do—can rest, well hidden and undisturbed, all day long.

The fluffy-feathered Boreal Owl is named for the northern forests in which it lives (boreal—of the North).

"Ears" That "Talk"

The funny tufts that stick up on the top of some owls' heads look like ears or horns, and they are usually called one or the other. In fact, they are just special feathers—but they do serve a purpose.

When an owl is resting quietly these feathers are only slightly raised above its head. The moment something upsets the owl, up shoot the feathery tufts.

If they stand up stiffly and a little forward, the owl is sending the same message a cat sends when it hunches its back and bushes out its tail: "I am ready to fight for what is mine."

Standing up but leaning slightly outward, the tufts send a less aggressive signal: "You have no business here, but I am prepared to put up with you as long as you behave."

And sometimes an owl that feels threatened will completely flatten the tufts, as if to say: "Don't mind me, I am just a little owl trying to get along."

Opposite page: It is easy to see how the Great Horned Owl came by its name. This one's "horns" are sending out a clear message: "Come any closer and there will be trouble."

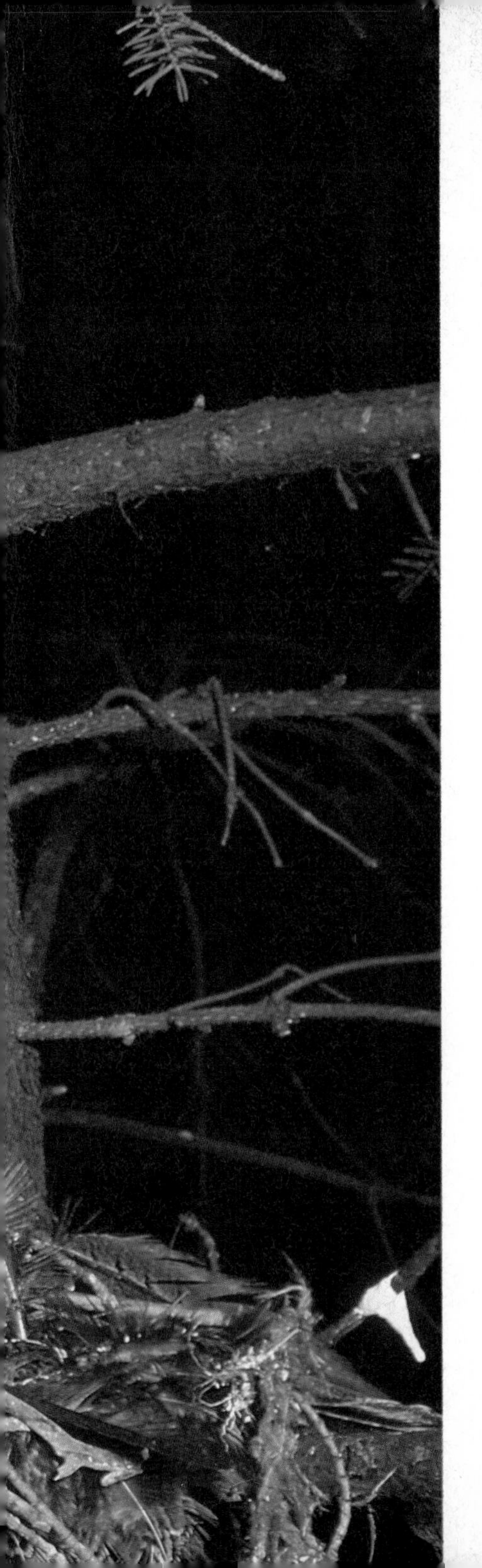

Owl Eyes

Have you ever tried to finish up a baseball game just as the last rays of evening light were fading into darkness? Remember how difficult it was to see the ball?

Dusk is the time of night when most owls start their hunting. How can they find tiny mice when it is too dark for us to see a large white baseball?

An owl's eyes are enormous. If the eyes in your head took up as much room as an owl's, each of your eyes would be the size of a GRAPEFRUIT! With such large eyes an owl can see much better in poor light than you can.

Owls' enormous eyes are especially equipped to catch the tiniest amounts of light. They are color-blind, however, and see everything in shades of gray. (Great Horned Owl and owlets)

But an owl cannot shift its large eyes from side to side the way you can. Its eyes are fixed in their sockets just like the headlights of a car. When an owl wants to look around it has to turn its whole head.

This is no problem for an owl, because underneath all those fluffy feathers it has a very long flexible neck. By twisting its neck, an owl can sit quite comfortably with its body pointed in one direction and its face in the other!

Many people think that owls cannot see well in daylight. Actually, they see as well in daylight as you do. But they are farsighted and do not see nearby objects clearly. In fact, day or night, an owl has trouble seeing its own feet.

Most birds close their eyes by raising their lower lid

Owls, however, lower their upper lid—just as you do.

An owl can turn its head around much farther and much more comfortably than you can turn yours—but it CANNOT turn it full circle. (Snowy Owl)

Hidden Ears

Owls could never wear earrings. Their ears do not stick out the way yours do. Instead, owls' ears are simply slits, sometimes very long, or small round holes on the sides of its head.

Even so, owls hear much better than you do. In fact, most owls hear so well that they can hunt just by listening for the tiny sounds a mouse makes as it scuttles about.

Some owls have lopsided ears—one larger and higher than the other. The sound of a mouse's movements will reach each of these ears at a slightly different time. From this difference an owl can tell exactly where the sound is coming from.

The special rings of curved feathers that surround each of the owl's eyes are called facial discs. These rings are very important to the owl because they help it hear. That's right: *hear.* The feathers in the facial discs are attached to muscles that control the shape of the ears. Just as a dog moves its ears to hear better, an owl moves these rings of feathers to locate sounds.

Opposite page: More than by anything else, we know an owl when we see one by the rings of curved feathers around its eyes. (Long-Eared Owl)

Swift and Silent

No matter how well an owl can see and hear, it would have a hard time catching anything if it sounded like a jumbo jet when it was flying.

To help muffle sounds, most owls' wings are well padded with soft, velvety feathers. The feathers along the leading edge of the wing are fringed just like the teeth on a comb. These fringed feathers also help to reduce the flapping noises that most birds make when they fly.

Try this simple experiment. Press the fingers of each hand tightly together and clap them against each other. Repeat the same thing with the fingers of both hands spread out. Much quieter, isn't it?

Like your outstretched fingers, the fringed edge of an owl's wing allows most of the air to pass right through. With their special wings, most owls can fly almost silently.

Most owls are fairly fast flyers. The Snowy, with its wing span of about 1.5 metres (5 feet), can work up to tremendous speeds, but it needs a long take-off and landing run.

Talented Toes

Apart from wiggling them, most of us do very little with our toes. Owls have many uses for their toes—perching, walking, grabbing, carrying.

All four of an owl's strong toes are equipped with hooked claws called talons. Just as you stretch your fingers out to catch a ball, owls can spread out their talons to make a successful strike.

Owls do this better than most birds because their outer toe is more movable. In fact, if they want to, they can even turn it right to the back so that it makes a pair with the back toe.

Owl's foot

This young Barred Owl has such a good grip on its perch that it is in no danger of falling off, even if it falls asleep.

Mice on the Menu

Would you eat in a restaurant that served gophers, mice and moths? You would if you were an owl. To an owl, such a menu would be DELICIOUS!

Owls never eat plants or bird seed. Meat is the only food that they can eat. The type of meat that an owl will eat depends upon how big the owl is and where it is hunting. A large owl that hunts in a meadow may eat lots of rabbits and mice. A small owl that hunts in a forest or desert may eat mice but will probably eat plenty of grasshoppers, moths and other insects as well.

Only insects and worms and the very smallest rodents have to worry about becoming a Pygmy Owl's dinner. The tiny Pygmy may weigh as little as 50 grams (2 ounces) and be no more than 13 centimetres (about 5 inches) long.

Lone Hunters

Many birds feed in large groups called flocks. To find enough food, owls need to hunt alone.

Take a minute to think of how you and your friends could collect the most eggs in an Easter egg hunt. Because the eggs are usually hidden in many different places, you would certainly find more if you spread out than if you grouped together.

Small rodents live all over the meadow and forest floor. By spreading out and hunting alone, each owl has a better chance of finding dinner.

On the watch for a likely lunch. (Hawk Owl)

A hunting owl will sit very still so as to surprise its prey. Perched high atop a tree, fence post or pile of rocks, an owl will wait—carefully watching and listening for rodents.

As soon as an owl has zeroed in on its meal, it swoops and pounces. The force of the pounce causes the owl's legs to bend and its talons to close.

A very hungry owl may have a picnic on the spot, but most will carry their dinner back to the safety of their perch.

Zeroed in...
(Short-Eared Owl)

A Neat Eater

Instead of picking the meat from the bones as you would when eating fried chicken, owls swallow fur, bones...everything! If the prey is small enough, they will even swallow it whole.

With owls, the work of sorting out what can be digested and what cannot goes on inside their stomach. Afterwards, the leftover bits are coughed up in a sausage-shaped pellet.

It may sound messy, but an owl pellet is actually very dry and neat. The tiny bits of bone and fur inside the pellet are just like pieces of a jigsaw puzzle. We can join enough of them back together to figure out what the owl has been eating.

Bull's-eye!
(Great Gray Owl)

Hard Times

It certainly seems that when it comes to hunting, the owl has all the advantages. But being a hunting owl is not always easy.

Like an unlucky fisherman, an owl may wait for hours without catching anything. On rainy evenings, in particular, many owls go hungry. The damp ground muffles the sounds rodents make, and it is hard for the owl to find them. Hunting is so difficult in the rain that most owls will sit out the storm and wait for better weather.

Most of the animals that owls hunt feed on plants. If a year is too cold or too dry, there will be fewer plants and therefore fewer rodents. At such times some owls will move to a new area to find food.

Barn Owls form a separate family of owls, and their heart-shaped faces and light coloring give them a quite distinctive look. Their name comes from the fact that they often nest in the dark corners of barns.

OWL
HOL

Who... Who... Who's There?

Every owl has its own section of forest or meadow that it calls home. The area is called the owl's territory.

Owls use a variety of calls to warn off unwelcome visitors. Some hoot, some whistle, and many have a call that resembles a shrill laugh. If you listen carefully on a clear night you might hear owls calling to each other. The owls in an area recognize one another by voice, and they know where their neighbors' territories are. As long as they are careful to hunt in their own backyards, the owls remain good neighbors.

This Burrowing Owl has staked out its territory on a golf course. It is not known whether the person who made the sign did so out of concern for the owl or the golfers.

Finding a Mate

In late January, a male owl's nightly calls will get louder and more frequent. This is mating season, and he is announcing his ownership of a territory in the hope of attracting females. Sometimes a female will answer with her own song, and the two will sing together in an owly duet.

Except for being a little bigger, most female owls look just like the males. Even a male owl sometimes has trouble telling the difference, and he is so protective of his territory that he may try to chase away the female he has worked so hard to attract. It often takes a lot of hooting and hollering before the male recognizes that the new bird is a female and not an unwelcome male.

To impress their new mates, male owls may perform trick flights or dance-like movements on a branch. And just as a man may send chocolates to his sweetheart, some male owls will woo their mates with gifts of tasty mice!

Some owls choose a new mate every year, but many stay together for life.

Opposite page: Unlike some owls, a male Snowy has no trouble knowing when he has attracted a female. She is easily recognizable by the dark marking on her feathers. Male Snowies are almost pure white.

Nesting Time

When it comes to nest building, owls lack talent. In fact, very few build nests at all. Instead, owls will lay their eggs in a hole in a tree, in a crack in a cliff, or in a slight hollow they scratch in the ground. Many owls will move into an abandoned nest that some other bird built the year before. There is even a Burrowing Owl that makes its home in the underground burrows of prairie dogs.

Some owls lay their eggs when the ground is still covered with snow. This may seem like a chilly time to start a family, but it means that the babies will hatch in spring—the time of year when there are lots of rodents to feed them.

Great Horned Owl

The older owlets will soon have to move out of the nest to give the younger ones room to hatch and grow. (Short-Eared Owlets)

Happy Hatch-Day!

A female owl may lay as few as 3 eggs or as many as 12. The number depends on the type of owl and on the amount of food available. An owl that is eating well will lay more eggs than one that is not.

The mother owl lays one egg and then waits a few days before laying the next. As a result, each egg hatches at a different time. Every baby owl, or owlet, has its very own hatch-day!

The eggs need both time and warmth to hatch. So, for several weeks, the father owl will hunt for two, while mom spends all her time sitting on the eggs to keep them warm. To do this more effectively, the mother owl will probably pluck out some of her feathers to make bare patches on her underbody. That is because the feathers that keep her warm would keep her body heat from reaching the eggs.

Hungry Babies

Except for two bare strips on its back, an owlet is covered in soft white feathers called down. With its back snuggled up to mom and this fluffy down to keep in the heat, the owlet stays cozy even in the chilliest storms.

Owlets grow very quickly and have huge appetites. A week-old owlet will eat much more for its size than an adult would.

The father owl is therefore kept very busy finding food for his family. Fortunately, owls are much better at catching mice than any cat. Even so, dad may end up having to hunt both night and day to keep up with the growing appetites.

Hungry owlets make soup-slurping noises when calling for their dinner. (Snowy owlet)

Devoted Parents

By three or four weeks of age, the baby's down is being replaced by longer gray and brownish feathers. The owlets now need so much food that their mother may leave them for short periods to help their father hunt. As the owlets grow, the increasing number of dark feathers help keep them well hidden while she is away.

Owls are very protective parents. If a hungry weasel or a curious person approaches the owlets, the parents will swoop down, threatening with their sharp talons. Even the tiny owlets help to scare off intruders by hissing, snapping their beaks and puffing up their feathery coats.

Long before they are able to fly, the young owlets move into the nearby branches and plants. Often people find these owlets, and thinking that they are lost, will take them home. The parent birds know where their babies are and are taking good care of them. It is important to leave them alone.

Keeping babies fed is a full-time job for dad.
(Burrowing Owl and owlet)

Growing Up

Owls learn to fly the same way that you learned to walk or to ride a bicycle—lots of practice and lots of bumps!

As the youngsters develop their flying skills, the parents will encourage them by dangling a tasty meal from a distance. Through practice, the young owls gradually learn to hunt for themselves. By fall it is time for them to leave their parents and set up territories of their own.

The first year of an owl's life is the most dangerous. With so much still to learn about the world, many of the young owls will not survive their first winter. But those that do live to celebrate their first hatch-day have a very good chance of living to celebrate many more.

By puffing out its feathers, this young Great Horned Owl is trying to look threatening and scare away an intruder.

Owls and Us

Owls are marvellous birds and helpful too! They help farmers by catching insects and rodents that like to eat their crops. Mice would be all over everything if there were no owls.

Because most owls are active at night, it is harder to watch them as they go about their daily routine than it is to watch other birds.

As a result, there are still many things we do not know about their ways and habits. So, the next time you are out in the woods, stop, take a careful look around, and give a few hoots. Who knows, you may be the next person to discover another fascinating fact about owls.

Happy Hooting!

Words to Know

Down Very soft, fluffy feathers.

Facial disc The ring of curved feathers that surround each of an owl's eyes.

Farsighted Able to see distant objects better than near ones.

Habitat The area or type of area in which an animal or plant naturally lives.

Hatch To break out of an egg.

Mating Season The time of year during which animals come together to produce young.

Order A grouping used in classifying animals and plants. An order is smaller than a *class* but larger than a *family*.

Owlet Baby owl.

Prey An animal hunted by another animal for food. A bird that hunts animals for food is often called a bird of prey.

Rodent An animal with teeth that are especially good for gnawing. Mice, rabbits and gophers are rodents.

Talon Claw of an owl, eagle or other bird of prey.

Territory Area that an animal or group of animals lives in and often defends from other animals of the same kind.

Tundra Flat land in the Arctic where no trees grow.

INDEX

Cover Photo: Stephen J. Krasemann (Valan Photos)
Photo credits: Wayne Lankinen (Valan Photos), pages 4, 8; Michel Julien (Valan Photos), pages 7, 19, 24, 28; Lowry Photo, pages, 11, 35; Ken Carmichael (Network Stock Photo File), pages 12, 32; Stephen J. Krasemann (Valan Photos), pages 15, 37, 42; Brian Morin, page 16; Albert Kuhnigk (Valan Photos), pages 20, 38, 44; Dennis W. Schmidt (Valan Photos), page 23; Brian Milne (Valan Photos), page 27; Federation of Ontario Naturalists, page 31; J.A. Wilkinson (Valan Photos), page 41.

Printed and Bound in Spain